# MYSTIC *River*

**POETRY**

**STACY NICHOLSON**

**Copyright © 2022 Stacy Nicholson**
Publisher is Hundred Faces of Love
Illustration: Dreamstime.com

All rights reserved. No part of this publication may be reproduced, stored, or transmitted in any form or by any means, electronic, mechanical, photocopying, recording, scanning, or otherwise without written permission from the publisher. It is illegal to copy this book, post it to a website, or distribute it by any other means without permission.

# MYSTIC *River*

**POETRY**

**STACY NICHOLSON**

## CONTENTS

**INTRODUCTION** .............................. 01

**LOVE POETRY** .............................. 03

*If I Could Be a Moon* ........................... 04
*Stay with Me* .................................. 05
*Bleeding Heart* ................................ 06
*Loved One* .................................... 08
*L'Amour* ...................................... 09
*For You* ....................................... 10
*Yearning* ...................................... 11
*Life Without Love* ............................. 12
*King of My Heart* .............................. 13
*Heart Whisper* ................................. 14
*Born for You* .................................. 16
*El Amor* ....................................... 17
*Amore Mio* .................................... 18

*Love Symphony* ................................ 20
*Desert Storm* .................................. 21
*Love Violin* .................................... 22
*Dominant* ..................................... 23
*Eternal Breath of Love* ......................... 24
*His Heart is My Home* ......................... 25
*Flower Fields* .................................. 26
*Forever* ....................................... 29
*Keep Loving Me* ............................... 30
*Winter Flower* ................................. 31
*Wild Heart Love* ............................... 32
*Unspoken* ..................................... 33
*Dreamer* ...................................... 34
*Symphony of Love* ............................. 35
*Red Rose's Petals* .............................. 36
*Our Love is Our Gift* .......................... 37

MYSTIC RIVER

| | |
|---|---|
| Love River | 38 |
| Eyes Filled With Stars | 39 |
| Love of My Life | 40 |

## LOSS POETRY ... 41

| | |
|---|---|
| Liberty Love | 42 |
| Albatross | 43 |
| Lovers Whisper | 44 |
| One-Sided Love | 45 |
| Should Trust You | 47 |
| Ruined Heart | 48 |
| Lost in Love | 49 |
| Silent Love | 51 |
| Love Window | 54 |
| Fatal Love | 55 |
| Split | 56 |
| Blanket of Silk | 57 |
| Man With a Black Heart | 59 |

| | |
|---|---|
| Dry Rose Petals | 60 |
| Buried in Snow | 62 |
| Our Love Is Our Rainbow | 64 |
| Day After Day | 66 |
| Still Loving You | 67 |
| Flambeaux | 68 |
| You Just Watched | 70 |
| Between God and Me | 71 |
| Broken Flower | 72 |

## GRIEF POETRY ... 73

| | |
|---|---|
| Ocean | 74 |
| Mystic River | 76 |
| Meteor | 78 |
| Little Bird | 80 |
| Between Dawn and Sunset | 81 |
| Life Verso Death | 84 |
| Broken Wings | 85 |

| | |
|---|---|
| *Sword* | *86* |
| *Child from a Black Night* | *87* |
| *Fragile* | *88* |
| *Rejected* | *90* |
| *Reborn* | *91* |
| *Place Without Love* | *93* |
| *Solitude* | *95* |
| *Labyrinth* | *97* |
| *Honey and Bees* | *99* |
| *In Search of Peace* | *100* |
| *Loneliness* | *101* |
| *Living Fearlessly* | *103* |
| *Nostalgia* | *106* |
| *Orange Desert* | *109* |
| *White Dove* | *111* |
| *Enchanted* | *112* |
| *Destined to Be Unloved* | *114* |

**SOLIDARITY POEMS** ......... **117**

| | |
|---|---|
| *Parallel Living* | *118* |
| *Trapped* | *120* |
| *Srebrenica: Bosnia and Herzegovina* | *122* |
| *In God's Hands* | *124* |
| *Fields of Wheat* | *126* |
| *If My Tears Could Realise My Pain* | *128* |

**ABOUT THE AUTHOR** ......... **131**

# INTRODUCTION

*Mystic River* is a collection of selected poems I have shared over the past two years on social media. Themes of poems vary in experiences ranging from love to pain. I wrote poems to bring light into people's lives where it is needed, and to strengthen their belief in love.

Writing is an important part of my life, and I use my pen to bring out diverse issues in society, such as mental health problems and the current situation of the world and humanity. When I write, I keep in mind a wide audience and tackle versatile topics.

My first poetry book, *Stay With Me*, targeted younger generations; *Mystic River* is a poetry book of poems to be loved and celebrated by different generations and identities.

Thank you for reading *Mystic River*. I hope you will love my poetry.

# LOVE POETRY

# IF I COULD BE A MOON

If I could be a moon in the night sky,
I could be surrounded by stars.
You would be mine forever, love.
I would be happy witnessing the beauty of the world
From far above . . .

If I could be a moon,
I would light flowers with sparks to decorate the grass.
I would colour all butterflies with rainbows of love.
I would spark rivers with millions of shining stars.
I would make an ocean of shining opals to decorate the Earth.

If I could be a moon,
The sky would be a silky, blue blanket of love.
You would be my silver, shining stars covering the sky.
You would light Earth with our love.
We would make magic together, all over the world.

Your love makes me see it all:
I do not need to be a moon after all.
I am already wrapped in your silky blanket of love.
You are my magic;
Your love makes all my dreams come alive.

# STAY WITH ME

In the most beautiful garden,
You are my flower
That outshines all other flowers—
One that is decorated with sun rays,
Watered from the well of my love.
Stars in the night sky can't compare
To your beauty and how
it shines your heart.
Because of you, I found myself again.
I started to live a life.
I will love you forever.
With each breath of air I take,
You will be the love of my life
As long as I am alive.

# BLEEDING HEART

Swaddle me in your loving embrace.
Keep my heart safe and sound.
Allow your touch to warm my heart.
Fan that fire to ignite that spark.

Blanket me in all your cuddles
As clouds over-blanket the sky.
Cover me with adorning grace;
Drape my frame in your elegance.

Sheath my soul enrichment
As sunlight brings back life.
Let the stars and moon be our wrapping—
Visible starlight a glowing shell of love.

Feel the gentleness from my heart; listen to its beats.
Feel and hear the sound of my love.
I will look inside your eyes because
I want to heal this bleeding heart.

# LOVED ONE

Your hands all over m;
Your love inside the deepest parts of my heart.
How beautiful is our love?
I cannot get enough of you.

What fire have you lit inside of me?
Making me wild and cuddly at the same time.
I drown in your arms.
I disappear and melt inside that body of yours!

I am a drop of water inside the palm of your hand.
You turn me into millions of rose petals,
Which disappear, evaporate into air,
With the touch of your breath on my face.

You complete me
In the most beautiful and special way.
I like you with every inch of myself.
I love you in the most special way.

There is no one like you in this world.
How lucky I am that you choose to love me!

# L'AMOUR

Touch me any way you want.
When I am with you,
Love speaks to me
In one million languages.
My heart understands all of them.
Wrap me in your silky blanket of love.
I want it to be the only feeling
I experience on my naked skin.
Let's use the fire of your heart to
Light days and night of our love.
Touch me with kisses, hands, eyes . . .
Touch me any way you want.
You are forever mon amour,
King of my heart.

# FOR YOU

I will let the sun dress me with its rays.
For you, I will shine.
I will let you kiss me
To witness glory of our love,
To see our greatness,
For you to treasure it forever.
Your heart is the place where
My true light is.
Do not forget that I lit this light—
For the magic of love to exist,
Two people are needed.

# YEARNING

Guide my heart
Into your oasis of love.
Do not make me live thirsty.
You are my well of life - my heart yearns
For your love.

# LIFE WITHOUT LOVE

Fill my heart with love
As a desert sun burns orange sand.
Let me burn inside your arms—
Awaken me to feel life
and being alive.
To me you are both sun and moon
And the millions of shining stars that cover night sky.
What is life without love?
It is a lost one.

# KING OF MY HEART

Without you, streets are empty,
Leading me nowhere.
Without you, destiny does not exist.
You are like a wind through my life,
A refresher on hard day,
And a sun that make rainbows
When the sky is dark and tries to hide.
You are the king of my heart.
I kneel in front of you
To receive the rays of your love,
Which make my dreams real and alive.

# HEART WHISPER

If my love could speak,
It would be a murmur of ocean waves,
a bird's tweet.
If my love could speak,
It would be the magic
That nature makes:
Sun rays falling with golden sparks on green grass;
Rainbow colours covering butterfly wings.
If only my love could speak,
It would find you where you are
To tell you how lonely my life is without you.
My love would tell you
How flowers bloom and stars cover the night sky.
You would understand the fire in my heart
And shine stars in your eyes.
If my love could speak,
It would be words that
Come from the depths of my heart
And the essence of who I am.
If my love could speak,
You would hear
Whispers of my heart
Echoing endlessly into the well of my desire

# BORN FOR YOU

I am born in the name of our love.
Because of our love, stars shine in the sky.
Because of our love, sun spreads warmth on flowers to bloom.
Your love makes all the beauty around me alive.
In the name of your love, I am born.

There are other loves that could be mine,
But stars did not have the energy from them to light the sky.
Flowers could not be warmed by these loves.
Only your love is true.

My soul writes songs in the blue sky about love,
Which shines for me from your eyes.
How I could love anyone but you?
Your love—the essence of my heart and soul,
And the reason I am born.
Each night my heart calls you to come back to me.

# EL AMOR

She sees flower fields inside his eyes.
El amor . . .
He holds her hand, but has her heart.
El amor . . .
He loves her the way she is.
El amor . . .
He sees her as nobody saw her before.
El amor . . .
He lets her be her true self—naked and wild.


He is her . . . El Amor.

# AMORE MIO

Only you, my love . . .
My sun rays from the sky.
Stars from the night sky.

Only you, my love . . .
You are my world and my life:
Amore Mio.

When my head falls
On your chest,
Your heartbeat is
The most beautiful sound of our love.

You are the tears of my heart.
The light of my eyes.
My breath of fresh air.
Amore Mio who makes
Flowers bloom from our love . . .

My fountain of happiness and my life:
Amore Mio.

# LOVE SYMPHONY

Making love with you is music:
Music orchestrated by our bodies.
Music dirigo by our love.
Making love with you became my symphony,
A symphony that will never be copied
It is always going to be done in original way,
Between you and me.
It is my love symphony.

# DESERT STORM

Burn me, my desert sun.
Your breath of air on my skin
Makes me fly.
Your breath of air is as powerful
As a desert wind
That makes me fly
Carried by the wings of our love,
I am becoming a burning desert wind, too.
Your kisses give me life,
Over and over, so I do not die.
Don't stop kissing me, my love.
While I am flying,
Our love is our awakening.

My burning desert sun,
Keep kissing me—do not stop.
Keep kissing me until the end of our time.

# LOVE VIOLIN

Play me—
I am your violin.
Your fingers touch
The strings of my heart.
Play me to make
The most beautiful songs of our love.
The most beautiful time for me
Is the time when I am inside your arms.
I do not care if it is day or night .
Play me whenever you want.
You are my forever love.
Your hands make magic,
Turning me into atoms of love.

Play me—
I am your violin.
Your fingers touch the strings of my heart.

# DOMINANT

With you, I am everything. Without you, I don't exist.
I am only an empty shell, or a star without shine.
You feed my heart and make my mind stronger.
You make me beautiful and enlightened.
My dream at night,
You are my heartbeats in life . . .
You fulfill me
By satisfying my body and my mind.
You love me with passion and devotion as no one has before.
I will love you up to my last breath,
And even when life starts leaving my body,
I will hold out hope that I will meet you again,
Somewhere between stars, in drops of rain,
In the breeze of air, or in ocean waves.
In flowers' whispers, my soul will find you;
It is never going to separate from you.
You are my life and dominant love.
You are my destiny.

# ETERNAL BREATH OF LOVE

Close your eyes, my love, from faraway land.
See lightning stars from my silver eyes.
Hear my whispering voice in the deepest dark,
From which the ocean comes.
Come to me on flowers' whispers made by the wind.
Bring me a blanket of blue silk with shining stars.
Steal it for me from the night sky.
Wrap me in it so I am the angel of your heart.
You've caught me while I'm flying through time:
I'm a silver star lost in the eternity of life.
Spread a net of love for my fall,
Because I am love of your life.
Find me in the bottom of the ocean,
Hidden inside the shell of love.
Take me in your hands and let me
Release the scent of woman in love.
What are we without each other?

Only incomplete halfs
On a journey to find true love.

# HIS HEART IS MY HOME

Finding peace inside his heart—
Did I break the lock,
Or did he let me in?
A forever mystery.
I am sure he will never let me know.
He does not even believe he had an opening.
But I could see it; I could feel it.
Now, I am in the place
Where I always wanted to be:
Inside his heart,
I found my forever home.

# FLOWER FIELDS

Find me,
Love me as you never loved
Any woman before me.
I will wait for you,
In the most beautiful of flower fields,
For you to make love with me.
On the petals of millions of red roses,
I will wait.

When I am with you, roses bloom all around me.
Our souls are destined to make love together.
Your heart is mine and can beat just for me.
In your life, no other woman will enter . . .
I will never let another woman be loved by you,
To take what is mine and belongs to me.

My life is mortal, but my love for you is forever.
I will love you up to the end of the time.
My love is breezes, sun rays,
And the most beautiful stars on night sky.
My love is a beautiful mystery
That exists only for you and me.

# FOREVER

With you, I learned what love is:
Rushes of blood running to cheeks
When your eyes gaze into mine,
When your kisses cover my lips,
Making my heart tremble happily.
Your love brought
Springs and flower whispers
Into my life.
My dreams turned into rainbows,
And you became my breath of air;
My whole life.
With you, I started to live a life.
In my heart, no other man will ever have a place.
My heart will be forever
Faithful to our love.

# KEEP LOVING ME

I love how your love makes me feel.
I love being naked in your arms.
I love when my heart burns

From your hands and eyes.
If your love is a river,
My heart is a well—keep filling it.
If your river doesn't have an end,
My heart doesn't have bottom.
Keep loving me . . . keep burning me . . .

# WINTER FLOWER

What would I give on this winter night,
Full of snowflakes and shining stars,
To have your lips softly touching mine,
Your hands touching my breasts,
Your arms wrapped around my waist, warming me.

What would I give tonight
To fall asleep on your chest
And wake up in the morning
As a crystal flower, which in glory
blooms under winter snow.

What would I give on this winter night,
Full of snowflakes and shining stars,
To have your love cover me as a blanket
of white snowflakes—
I, as a winter flower instead of snow,
Would rise under the blanket of your love.

What would I give
To wake up in the morning
To your eyes instead of the sun
Showering me with love and millions of golden sparks.
I dream of this white winter night, full of snowflakes and stars,
Where I am your majestic flower, which blooms
under the blanket of your love instead of snow.

# WILD HEART LOVE

When your eyes gaze into mine,
They make love all over me.
Everything that is beautiful in this world comes alive
The moment your eyes gaze inside mine.

When your eyes gaze into mine,
Heaven opens the door for me.
My heart is whispering songs of our love
The moment your eyes gaze into mine.

When your eyes gaze into mine,
It's just the two of us.
Our hearts surrender to each other,
The moment your eyes gaze into mine.

When your eyes gaze into mine,
They bring me to this very special moment,
When my heart started to beat in rhythm with yours,
The moment when you got my wild heart love—
The very first moment when your eyes gazed into mine.

# UNSPOKEN

What kind of woman am I in your dreams?
Do you see me running barefoot through flower fields?
Is my long hair full of butterflies or shining stars?
What kind of woman am I when you close your eyes?


What kind of dream am I to you?
Am I white silk or black lace wrapped inside your sheets?
Am I naked, showered in sun rays and golden beams?
Do I wear a white dress and run between wildflower fields?

What kind of life do I live inside your dreams?
Is it a wild one where you let me be free?
Do I carry a sword in my arms?
Am I power, or your gentle flower?

Do you hold me in your arms,
In bed full of red roses, where everything is real
but still just a dream?
Do you like just to dream, or you are planning to make it real?

# DREAMER

I will enter inside your mind
To extinguish fires of my love and satisfy woman's desire,
To take the challenge in love and dominate man.
I choose you to be the one, the man of my night.

I will open the door of life, and you will be my window of love.
I will spread the magic called love and man's fire and desire.
I will bring light and power inside your night.
Your heart will burn and become ashes from my burning flame.

I will shake feelings and emotion inside your heart and mind.
Your clouds of darkness will be destroyed.
I will break your chains,
Leave you to live with only the link of my love.

I will rupture your feelings and make you burn.
I will stop you from being dreamer and seeing angels from sky.
I will let you get a feel of me, a real life angel,
To forget one from sky.

# SYMPHONY OF LOVE

Sex with you is to dream of us making love.
It is the stopping of time, where two hearts celebrate love.
Two bodies move and make themselves into one.

Sex with you is my never-ending symphony of love.
Because of its quality, I want it to be played over and over again.
I rewind our symphony to be played again and again and again.
Sex with you only makes my body more thirsty for your love.

You get inside me as a river gets inside an ocean.
My heart can't ever get enough of you or your love.
I want our symphony to last until the end of time.

# RED ROSE'S PETALS

Love of mine, are you traveling along beautiful, blue sky,
Or are you nesting in powerful blue ocean waves,
Conquering the world and hiding the sun
When night starts falling,
Then remake the sky in burning colours
of our powerful love?

To where did you fly away from me, my love?
To which side of world did wind pull you away,
To hide from my heart?
Where are you now—in sun rays,
Or in petals of red roses, with your beauty
Decorating the world?

Did you find another home and now nest
With some other couple, giving them a pillow of love?
What happened to your magic and power that once ruled my life?
Did you, my love, decide to nest in some other woman's heart?
Is this why you left me, my mystery love?
How did you fly away . . .
How did I let you go, my love . . .
What happened to me?

It has to be that stars in the night stole you away
With their eternal shine.
Whatever happened, I want to believe that in petals of roses,
You found your forever home, and instead of my life now,
You decorate a whole world with the magic colours
Of our mysterious love.
Our Love is Our Gift

# OUR LOVE IS OUR GIFT

Open your heart—
Let me mend whatever
Is broken and painful.
Let my heart become your home.
My love will help you get carried away.

Whatever has become heavy,
Let my love be your shield
And your forever light.
Love is a gift, and people get matched

For reasons or destiny—the universe decides.
Or God himself, who sees two hearts,
Decides to make them into one,
To gift them the joy of love.

# LOVE RIVER

My Love River gently curves its flow
Around your love.
That river in the depths of my heart
Finds its way towards you
To connect with your love.
The river that is untamed, wild and full of sunny sparks.
The river that flows and moves under the power of my love.
It is an unpredictable river;
I am never sure if it will cover me with its sparks,
Wrap my heart into glittering stars,
Or swallow me into the dangerous depth
Of my secret passions and desires.
The only thing that I am sure of is that,
As other rivers flow towards the ocean,
Towards their destiny,
My Love River flows towards its destiny,
Towards you, my love ,
Jewel of my heart,
In search of your love . . .
On a mission to conquer your heart and make it mine.
My Love River is on track
To make the world become mine.
My Love River is on task,
Connecting your love with mine

# EYES FILLED WITH STARS

Even though you are far away,
I still know that inside of you is the burning
Flame of our love,
The flame of love I lit inside your heart.
I know that you still love me . . .
I know that time did not extinguish
What we had between the two of us.

I know so much about life, yet so little about love
And the fantasies you write about me.
Still, my heart does not ask you questions.
When our eyes meet,
Every question loses meaning,
Every thought gets lost
Inside the infinity of our love.

Your loving eyes and the hidden world there
Opens the gates of love for me.
Your magic eyes invite my life path
Cross with yours,
And nothing needs to be asked or said.
I know I love you
With the burning passion of my heart
And that you love me, too, with passion and light.
Even the sun can't outshine
All the sparks and stars we can see
When we look inside each other's eyes.

# LOVE OF MY LIFE

I love you with the purity of my heart.
I love you with light from my eyes.
I love you with my whole heart.
I love you with my soul, the essence of who I am.

I find you through love, which shines for me
From depth of your eyes.
I find you in each breath of air I take.
Love has nestled you into the depths of my heart.

You are my whole world and the light of my life.
Without you, love would not exist.
Without you, flowers would lose
their colours and become dull blooms.

Without you, I am nothing.
With you, I am everything.
If you are the sun, I am the moon.
If you are sky, I am your shining star.

If you are my love, I am your life.
If I am your life, you are my heart
If you are my heart, I am your powerful beats.
If I am your heart beats, you are my blood.

Our love unites us as one.
We will love each other until the end of time.

# LOSS POETRY

# LIBERTY LOVE

I will let you go . . . I will free you . . .
Be an eagle; spread your wings and fly in the sky.
Let our love be a kite, carried by wind of time.
I will let my heart suffer and cry.
I will do anything for you . . .
I will do anything to find a way inside your heart,
To open the door for our love.
As a sunset as a dawn my love for you rises and falls
But I only see what is between:
Beautiful rainbows and magic of colours,
Mystery shadows of our love.
My desires raise up to the sky
And nestle between shining stars.
I will always see your love everywhere.
I will hear your whispers from all sides of world,
No matter where you are.
From west to east, from south to north,
My love will come from deepest part of my heart;
It will speak to my soul, too.
Your love will always find me wherever you are.
From west to east, from north to south.
In the rising and falling of the sun, I will see your love . . .
Time and distance mean nothing.
Our love only has one nest, only one home.
You will come back to me, too, so in my heart
Is our love and your home.
I let you fly because I know
You will always come back to me . . .
"To your one and only love."

# ALBATROSS

While in sorrow, I live and breathe.
The only thing that keeps me alive
Is knowing we will meet again,
That our paths will cross once more.
Somewhere far away, where stars spark the night sky.
One place where my loneliness will be crashed
and forever broken.

As my love burns, I wonder if yours is still alive.
Do you think about me?
Do you touch me in your dreams?
Do you fly with me on wings of love?
Do our hearts meet in your far away dreams?
There are so many wonders in the love between the two of us . . .

Are you waiting for me?
Do my kisses touch you when I send them to you?
I wonder and wonder . . .
Each night my heart and mind pray to reach your heart.
Then life paths would open to us,
And you would come to me
To stop my lonely nights . . . to stop your lonely nights, too.

Your love is magic; it can turn the world around.
It can turn my life around.
Black duckling, crying swan . . . what am I?
I am an albatross who waits for your love to empower my wings
To fly across the sky.

# LOVERS WHISPER

Lovers whisper, breaking the silence.
Their crying sounds fly to each other, carried by the breeze of wind.
Across the ocean and many mountains high, whispers fly:
How far to each other we become: whispers-whisper???

Birdsong covers the night sky ,
Their singing calling lonely lovers' hearts:
Come to each other and celebrate
What humans are calling beauty and love.

The sun slowly disappears into the orange pool, making rainbows
On an empty horizon of love.
Blue clouds are sprinkling flower petals of love
With tears of angels,
To acknowledge a loss of love, which was a gift from the sky.

He desperately calls to her: come to me, darling, inside my arms.
She points her sad eyes towards the empty sky:
No stars shine that night.
Everything that nature could bring to life
In the night cried.
Because lovers' hearts are now separated.

# ONE-SIDED LOVE

Watch the dark blue sky
And how it cries.
It's fire and lighting
For love that is forever lost ,
Love flames, raised into the sky . . .
Witness the sea washing our pieces of love along the shore.
Does not it make you wonder what we are?
We will disappear together with our loves.
Stories will stay, but lives will get lost.
What did I do or not do
To keep my place inside your heart?
How our love got broken in pieces and died !
I can understand these storms,
Lighting, and ocean waves,
But I can't understand
How love dies in your heart, forever
Extinguished from your eyes.
If I only could collect it like shells lost in sand.
If I could do anything to get you back . . .
If magic that was once inside our eyes
Still had fireflies,
I could make it burn again.
But everything has died, crashed
Into pieces by the waves of our lives.
Only the memories survive.
A memory of our love . . .
I am never going to forget you,
My one and only, forever lost, love.

I am never going to forget our story of love.
In my heart, it is never going to die . . .
Even though I know that in your life I was
A drop of rain swallowed by an endless blue sea,
Crashed and lost forever
To the waves and storms of your life.

# SHOULD TRUST YOU

Your love, a burning flame of passion in the air, and lightning from the stars—
Love that burned with pleasure in my soul and my heart.
My love for you was a dangerous, deadly swirl of flames;
Love I should not desire to be mine.
I knew your heart of stone would not return my feelings of love for you.

Still, love entered into me as a dangerously provoked ocean wave,
Destroying me, but also allowing me to see and experience the magic.
Love should be enjoyed just for a short moment of time.
I still tried to catch and keep it, to crash this heart of stone inside you . . .

It was my desperation to keep this power of love
I felt for the first time in my life.
Your maturity was enchanted by my youth and beauty,
But it did not lust for a long time.

It did not take long for you to decide you were better on your own.
My beauty and youth for your mature age was not enough.
On my knees, I pleaded with God for one more night of your love.
That night, I was not even worth enough to turn your head back on me.

Only rain from the sky sided with my lonely heart,
To acknowledge the loss of love I felt for the first time.
Rain tried to help me to extinguish this love flame,
which still burned inside me with power, even while you were leaving.

I swear through lonely nights that I will not ever love again—
But what is the point?
When we met, you told me that your heart was not for love.
I should have trusted so for you it was lust, and for me, pure love.

# RUINED HEART

A lot of dreams get lost inside impossible love,
A love where hearts are too different and cannot be matched.

Too many tears and not much happiness live this love,
Until my heart finally lost the strength to love and decided to say goodbye,
To let lost love be free, and release it to fly to faraway skies.
Millions of treasured love pieces get lost in the sky;
Only God knows where they fly.

Love, which never was alive, but the heart refused to separate from,
Refused to believe what was real instead of the biggest and beautiful dream.

This love remains a black shadow in my life,
Swallowing any happiness life could have.
It prevents any dream from being born again,
So the wounded heart refuses to heal and love again.

## LOST IN LOVE

I still dream about a time between the two of us
When I believed in love.
When I believed in you, in us.
Dreams slowly disappeared
Inside tears and lonely nights.
I have to accept that what we had was not true love;
It was desire for something powerful and different
To bring to life and destroy lonely nights.
This is what you were in my life.
Now, in sunsets, the sun hides behind clouds.
These feelings for you
Get slowly lost in the orange-coloured sky.
The memory of the two of us is disappearing.
In the midst of our lives,
These powerful emotions slowly get lost
As autumn leaves my wishes unfulfilled
And love unreturned.
I fly somewhere far away,
Not to be recovered or found ever again.
I am seeing slowly only the shadows
Of what my heart once called love,
What my mind desired and my heart cried for . . .
What my poetry verses called love.

# SILENT LOVE

Silent love inside a powerful burning heart.
Soul desiring to be touched, to be discovered,
To stop loneliness . . . to be touched
By love from your eyes as it was once.
Still, I know it will never happen again,
As powerfully burned as it was, with the same power, it was destroyed.

My love was wildflower fields that bloomed in my mind
When I met your eyes,
When your smile touched my soul and my heart.
I'll never forget this time . . . still, it's hard to remember.
How is a heart to cope with betrayal
When I discovered that I meant nothing to you?

My feelings of love were a breeze in the faraway sky,
Still locked in the deepest parts of my heart.
I would give everything for you, but you still left me.
My crying meant nothing to you.
For me, our love was a dream, a piece of heaven I stole from the sky.
For you, it was a short stop on your travel
Through life as you aimed to reach the sky.

My eyes are dry, but my heart cries.
Love still sustains in me. From ruins of my heart grow again,
but I do not want anyone to love again.
I do not want love to grow all over again.
Pieces of the dream you left behind is enough for me.
I lived it once, so I do not need it anymore.

In my life, nothing was real.
Your love was not real, either.
I was always a giver, and you were the biggest taker.
You damaged the only thing that was mine and pure.
You damaged my heart and destroyed my dreams—
The only thing in life that I treasured, and that was mine.

# LOVE WINDOW

Rain, rain my heart. Weep my soul.
You have the right to show that you are in pain.
For love you desire, but hurt you have lived.

There was no street
That could lead you to his heart
Or into his mind.
He closed all gates that led to love.

At some point in my life, we met.
At some point in my life, we parted forever.
No love left. No love existed.
He was a piece of dream I wanted to live.

Acquaintances, but not lovers.
Not a couple in love.
Not destined to live powerful feelings that would fly
In the air between us.

Love flew, but never nested, in his heart.
I met him just to say one final "Goodbye";
Memory and imagination show me
What it could have been between us.

Looking now through a window into my life,
I can see him passing through time,
Just as I see my own life passing.
Just as flowers dry without blooming,
My love for him passed over seasons.

Love that never flourished.
Love that never bloomed.
Love lost forever to the passing of time.

# FATAL LOVE

Listen to the silence of night.
Hear whispers of love,
Love that disappeared the same
As drops of rain falling and disappearing inside green grass . . .
The same as our love disappearing inside time . . .
Only love whispers survive to stay, to break the silence of lonely nights.

Our love got lost in time
While, in screams, I lived through dark nights.
Still lonely, my heart calls you to come back.
Bring me sunshine, bring me a breeze on a heavy day.
Bring the flowers' colours and make the sun shine and warm the sky again.
Come back again, or my eyes will never dry . . .
My lonely heart cries through dark nights.

Beautiful clouds of blue colour decorate the sky still,
Awakening my desire for you and your love,
Awakening my wish for your love to come alive again.
Love, I feel for you, for taking my life, but then again,
without you, I do not feel alive . . .
I feel like I died with our love.

In whisper of flowing rivers lost in the horizons of life,
In gentle butterflies lost
Between flowers and the breeze,
My heartbeat became lost, too.
Love leaving me was like the sun hiding behind dark sky.
Everything that had colours in my life in only one night
Became forever dull and dry.

# SPLIT

Your words sunburn and blister my heart.
Your words, once honey on my lips,
Now taste bitter, overpowering everything else.
Once you were my biggest love; now you are biggest sorrow.

In my life, everything is double-sided:
My beauty is my curse.
My strength is my pain.
My love is my sorrow.
My living is split between happiness and unhappiness.
My life is split between lives of
One who is dead and one who is alive.

My time of living is split between time loving you
And time trying to destroy this powerful love.
My love becomes my biggest sorrow,
which overpowers all other life sorrows.

My life is a never-ending battle with my love for you.
A battle without a winner ever to be announced.
A battle that will not have winner, ever.

I am woman split by time of living.
I am woman without life.
I breathe air, but I do not have life.
I am split.

# DRY ROSE PETALS

If my life could be
A river flowing into an ocean of infinity,
It would find you and reach to you again.
My love would find you wherever you are.

If my heart was a piece of stone,
It would love you with the same fire again -
It is how powerful my love is.
Still, if I could be born again,
I would ask only not to love
So all my rivers flow towards the dreams where love lives.
This is where and how the dreams become lost.
My love river, which flows towards you,
Was the strongest one.
It was so strong, it made me live my life lost.

The only things I remember now
Are the dangers and life swirls it brought me into.
Now my life is a dry river bed.
My heart is full of cracks and scars as reminders
That it was alive once,
And that my life river once flowed.
Now my life, my dry river bed,
Is a reminder of the pain and sorrow
That stayed behind.

# MAN WITH A BLACK HEART

Black pain and grey suffering.
Black days and even more black years.
It is what's left, after you left me.

Even though the blackness faded
And the sun later came,
I could not feel warm in my life
Or heart anymore.

Pain and dark nights that followed our love
Caused distraction of its own.
Everything that was beautiful in me
Slowly died inside the dark and without sun.
Without the sun, without your love,
I was not able to breathe anymore.

My constant fights to take a breath of air
And not drown in a sea of pain,
Trying to erase memories of you,
Became my regular life of struggles and fights,
Which I won and survived.

I won and survived,
But it is snowing in my heart now.
It is winter in my life forever.
Spring will never come in my heart or mind again.
Nothing will blossom in my life after you.

It took years for my love to fade.
It took years for my love to stop breathing.
When love left me, you remained in my life
As the man with black heart who
Sucked everything from me and left me
Inside deep dark night to die.

# BLANKET OF SILK

Cry my soul ,try to heal .
Let sadness out from inside my heart.
My love is one endless teardrop from sky . . .
Will he ever remember our love?
Does he remember when stars inside our eyes
Could light up the sky?
When love was everything we needed
And it ruled our lives?
I still feel touches of his eyes on my skin.
Like a silk blanket, he covered me with his love.
Silk blanket, breezes of love from his eyes.
Now my heart does not want to let it go.
It wants to make it alive again-
To make alive a love that died years ago
And existed in some other time . . .
I am rambling through darkness
In search of a light that will never shine again . . .
For stars that were extinguished in time and died.
If only memories could disappear from our lives
As everything else does . . .
Then I would not be hopeless anymore.
The silk blanket and the memory of his love
Would be burned by the time of
Our lives.

My black destiny took everything
That I ever loved and lived for ,
At the end, let me look at
How my life flew and disappeared with time.
Let me witness my life as torn, dried rose petals
Getting carried by the wind to all four corners of the world.
This is what my life after loving has become.

Destiny - my black destiny ,decided that
Nothing will ever flourish from my loves.

# BURIED IN SNOW

My feelings of love are the most beautiful sun rays and stars from the sky.
My soul is buried in the deepest snow because of my love for him.
I am frozen, shaken, overpowered by this love flame.
I want to throw myself. I want to throw my love for him.

Nothing about my love makes sense.
How can I love a man with a black heart?
I hate him, but with same power that I love him.
My life is running from myself and then being stuck with him.
How can I face the truth that he will never love me?
I am just a spark of last in his mind,
A piece of something to be used and thrown in a faraway sky.

Where am I to run? Where am I to hide from myself?
He owns every part of me—my soul and my heart.
If there was a way to end this love, I would find it.
If I could stop breathing and end it like that, I would.
It is life that makes a sarcastic game of me.
I prayed for love, but now I would do anything to free myself from it.

Under deep snow, my heart is frozen and my soul lies buried.
Still, my love for him is untouched.

As cruel as he is, he assures that even without him,
The flame of love will burn and make me suffer forever.
At the end it's probably not about him, but about me.
I think it's my destiny to die hopelessly being in love.

# OUR LOVE IS OUR RAINBOW

Our love was a beautiful rainbow
With the most beautiful colours
Decorating our lives.
It came after the rain of sadness we had been covered with.


As the sun started to warm our lives,
Our love disappeared .
Desires for this love left me,
Making me see reminders
Of you in everything around me,
Reminders that did not allow me to move on with my life.

In the ocean's whispers, I can hear your heartbeat.
Wind whispers your name to me.
In faraway sky, I see our love.
I see the ashes of our love covering the blue sky.

The fire of our love is extinguished, but the smoke is still there.
I can't breathe fully anymore.
I point my eyes towards the faraway sky
To pray, to look for the salvation this love reminders.
Then I remember what it felt like to once be
So happy and in love.

My heart does not want to let you go.
I remember the colours of love,
Same as rainbow that striped our lives.
You entered places of my heart
That had never been touched before—
The essence of me.

You made me fall in love, and then you left me, saying:
*Love is not for you.*
*There are other things that defined us.*

My heart left exposed.
My life became lost.
I became a wounded bird.
The only thing left for me was to die.
You destroyed the essence of me.
My life became a shadow of the rainbow that
Cried for the most beautiful colours of life
That striped my life once upon a time.

# DAY AFTER DAY

Day after day,
My love, I try to find you wherever you are.
Like rain from the sky, I dream of putting drops of my love
On your heart, to be sucked inside your mind.
I imagine you as a blue sky,
Then I cover you with millions of shining stars.

Day after day
You continue to be my dream.
You become powerful love magic made in this surreal life,
Which shines at night while I am living this hard life.
I let you root deep inside my heart,
Then I fall hopelessly in love with you.

Day after day
This powerful dream is a crashing mirror of my sadness,
But it means nothing to me. I live in my loneliness.
I should turn a new page and walk away,
Live life as all other people do.
Still I follow my heart and refuse to listen to my mind.

I live in dreams where nothing in life is real.

# STILL LOVING YOU

I wish there were words
That could speak my sorrow.
I wish there were words
That could speak my love to you . . .
But everything is stacked inside my heart.
Everything gets said
With fire and tears from my eyes . . .
What is there to say after all?
You will never understand the pain
I carry inside my wounded heart.
You did not see the arrows of pain
That get stuck inside my heart,
Carried there until I die.
You will never understand
The strength I bear to inhale air,
To let love not die,
To continue to love you every day,
Every morning when I wake up.
You can't understand, because you only witness
My failures, but not my strength as I live my life.
You cannot understand something you have not lived ,
Yet you judge me and blame my heart,
Which would die for you.

# FLAMBEAUX

Forever winter is in this place
Where her lost and isolated soul finally found home.
Her desperate heart weeps for drops of love,
For loneliness to be crashed,
While her soul strives not to freeze and stay alive.

Sorrow took over her life,
Brought white winter into her black nights.
Her soul became buried forever in snow so white.
Her freezing soul breathed without any sun to get warm.

Loneliness swallows her whole life,
Separates her from loved ones.
Life is torn apart and blows her to live
Isolated from everyone she ever loved.

In the depths of dark and cold nights, her lonely heart cries
With a soundless whisper of sorrow.
It calls life to bring the sun again.
It prays to God for stars to appear on the night sky.

Only hope lives inside her desperation—
Hope that never dies.
Hope that lights and burns as a flambeaux.
Hope that her eyes will meet his again.
Hope that she will touch the life she lived once before,

That she will be warm again,
From a sun shining from his eyes:
A flambeaux of her life; a memory of his love,
Flashing through her lonely, cold, dark nights.

Love flambeaux that does not melt the snow of loneliness
Does not bring stars out in the sky.
Her desperate heart imagined this flambeaux
To warm her on cold and lonely nights.


Desperate , desperate ,desperate , She,
The one imagining a flambeaux of his love,
To bring light and warmth into her lonely,
Enchanted life.

# YOU JUST WATCHED

Look for me in the faraway sky,
In clouds of fog where mountains disappear in the air,
In the tweets of birds and in rainbows.
Look for my love everywhere.

When we are not together,
I am nowhere and everywhere.
When we are not together,
My heart cries with tears from my eyes.

When we are not together,
I am the atoms in the air and drops of rain in a faraway sky.
It is my love that you made into teardrops
To water the grass and flowers.

I will always remember this moment in time
When I smiled and walked ahead,
But in my heart, I cried and pleaded for you to take my hand
And ask me to stay . . .

But you just watched me to walk away.

# BETWEEN GOD AND ME

My dear God, I believe in you so.
I bend my head and pray for flowers to get rainbow colours.
I raise my hands to reach the sun to warm the whole world.
I cry with crystal pearls from my eyes
To wash pain from each heart.

My dear God,
My heart and mind opened to his heart.
What connection of hearts has been made?
I do not understand this strangest way of life,
Where you decided to match our two hearts.

My dear God,
I question my destiny, and each day I ask myself: why?
The only thing I ever wanted was a drop of my mother's love.
Then I met him
And I wanted for myself a moment of love
Between me and him.

My dear God,
Now, I take a flower crown from my head and bend on my knees
So I am woman and not a child anymore.
I raise my hands and pray for the souls of both of us.
He chose not to love, and paid the price of a lonely life;
I chose to love and paid an even bigger price:
My soul wounded and hurt,
I lost the only life I believed in that was mine.

All of this was because of love . . .

# BROKEN FLOWER

Broken flower I am.
Mend me.

Do not touch the wounds
Inside my wounded heart;
They made me in who I am.
My wounded heart
Survived all these cuts—
It is still alive.
Love me the way I am,
Broken and wounded.
Feed me, and I will bloom
From your love again.

But a heart never fully healed will create
Wounds so deep, they split it in half.

# GRIEF POETRY

# OCEAN

The ocean covers most of the Earth.
It destroyed the world once,
And it is threatening with its waves to do so again.
Ocean, power of nature! Ocean, power made by God himself!

I am a human, a grain of sand carried by the waves.
I am a simple woman who lives but for a moment, then dies.
Above all, I am a woman,
But still I have all of the ocean inside myself.

My ocean—
Sometimes it is crystal clear and full of stars.
Sometimes it is dark and deep without an end.
And in this deep dark is whole mystery:
A beautiful pearl—my heart, my treasure.

When I was a child, these powerful waves ruled my life.
Powerful waves crushed me inside.
I felt pain, but I also felt power.

My ocean, my power:
Powerful waves managed by my soul—
A double-edged knife.
In order to survive, I had to learn how to muster that strength,
Not be killed by the powers I carried inside me.

When my soul cried or loved or felt the wind of life,
That was when it made waves.

The ocean sparked and lit my deepest dark places
And hepled me survive all storms in my life.

Everybody sees these waves inside me,
Sometimes full of sparking diamonds,
Sometimes full of darkness—
My power, my waves.


Who can understand humanity or how the ocean is made?
Or the essence of us that made us who we are?

# MYSTIC RIVER

My life is flowing and disappearing.
My dreams are flowing and disappearing.

My life is like a piece of wood that flows in a mystic river.
It is going somewhere far—who knows where?
A piece of wood, slowly disappearing along
The flow of this green river.

Rarely is my own water clear.
Rarely is there a reflection of sun sparkling in this river.
Just as in life, rarely is something clear,
And there is rarely a spark of light.

Mystic river, full of the dangerous swirls
This piece of wood is caught in.
Just as in life, I am caught in dangerous swirls all the time.
To survive and not drown,
I hold my breath for a while.
When I am finally out and everything starts to be normal,
I slowly start to breathe again.

My life is a piece of wood inside a dangerous green river,
Which I call the mystic river.
I do not understand how I am not crushed and destroyed.
It does not make sense, then, that I am destined to
Enter into the ocean and disappear there.

My sense of longing and belonging are constant.
My tears are streaming all the time down my face.
I wish to stand again, at this place next to the river where I once flowed,
To remind myself
Of when I was not hurt and crushed inside my heart,
To bring myself to a time
When I believed the river would bring me
To a beautiful place full of sparks and light.

Powerful feelings of longing and belonging
For this place of innocence,
Which does not exist anymore.
However, the mystic green river is still there, and flowing.

# METEOR

My life:
Soundless strings of violins cry,
It makes all flowers dry . . . it makes lovers cry . . .
It is so sad, my life . . .

The soundless whisper of my soul that
Flies along the sky, carrying my life, getting lost in time.
My life, my violin:
Music of my soul plays the strings of my heart
In the hopes that my cry will reach a place
Where it will not be lost.
My life, my violin:
Carrying hope that
Maybe it will find and join some
Other lonely star in the blue sky.
My life, my violin . . .
My lonely soul plays a song:
How I could be born
Where I do not have a place
I could call a home?
It must be I am a meteor who fell from the sky,
Got forever lost in time . . .
Lost in a place where it does not belong.
This must be the reason that, in my lonely nights,
My eyes look to the night sky,
Decorated with shining stars.
It must be that my real home is there
Between other shining stars . . .

Since I fell from the sky, separated from other stars,
I lost my shine.

My lonely heart lost its shine and become
Crying peace of stone get lost on earth
Without home....

# LITTLE BIRD

The saddest song is my life,
Like the murmur from millions of autumn leaves
Falling from the trees.
Orange leaves get carried by wind
To a faraway land
To disappear in time , to melt into the soil and die.
Like walking through a dark tunnel,
This is the way of living my life.
I am trying to find sparks
Of stars and to get warm from the sun,
But it is only a labyrinth
Wherever I go; I do not see sun in the sky,
Or stars at night.
What have I done to get lost in time?
Why did I finish in the dark night?
Everything is lost in fog:
Sun, stars, flowers, trees . . .
Nothing breathes around me.
How I am to live my life?
I feel like a fledgling that got lost,
A little bird that fell out of its mother's nest.

I try to fly .
I am not a bird, I know .
Though it is my way of desperation because

I am so small and lost.

# BETWEEN DAWN AND SUNSET

Shadows of love, pain, sadness, and many other shadows of life fly around us.
We are trying to escape from being hunted, so we living by running.
We run—trying to meet happiness and find love.
Many shadows follow us wherever we go.
Only one shadow, the shadow of love, once when it is found out,
Does not follow us, but is carried inside our heart
Throughout the time of our living.

The places where love starts, where love disappears,
Where our tears get wiped by time,
Where we celebrate our life
And everything we learn while living—what we achieve and even lose . . .
When we find this special place and stop running,
We stand there and forget the other shadows in each other to reflect
On what we lost and what we've gained over time.

To be able to rise above these reflections,
Above pain and loss, we do our best
To catch happiness and keep it forever with us,
Locked inside our hearts. We give our best, too,
Then we witness how the sun hides behind the horizon,
And everything starts disappearing slowly in front of our eyes.
Our shadows disappear, too, when the sun is gone . . .
Our life disappears inside a moment of time, then
We discover we are dying in this place where we found
The Answers and finally stopped running.

At the end, we conclude that we lost everything we could lose,
Because we spend our life running, not giving ourselves a chance
To forget the shadows and enjoy the moments of life
That get lost in our constant running,
Trying to catch these unreal shadows
That were only our imagination and a reflection
Of our attempts to make living meaningful.

We do not catch anything in the end.
Everything stayed behind us, lost in our constant running.
We become only memory, which soon will disappear, too.
Same as the shadows that disappear without a trace,
We will disappear, and the memory of our lives will disappear.
Everything will disappear, and once again when sun comes out,
New life will be born to start running all over,
To hunt shadows and happiness,
To find a place to stop and find the answers
About life and living . . .
Until then it is time to die and await the new life to be born
And start living all over again.

# LIFE VERSO DEATH

Between wondering about the sun rising and where the sun hides,
We are living life, we are finding love;
We escape pain, conquer life, and find salvation,
The salvation we desire to overcome pain and heavy temptations.

Some of us find it in love, some in kindness, some reach
To bad deeds to destroy faith, which did not assure light for life,
Then let it become a dark night without the moon or stars.
Some get lucky so not much darkness will be inside their lives.

Some find salvation waking heavy steps through darkness.
Some spend life looking for it and never reach a final destination.
Their hearts drown and get lost in the dark.
They get stacked forever in their own graveyard night.
Alive or dead for them, life becomes the same,
No salvation path open to them.

Life gets born—birth, wonder—life finishes—death, wonder.
The two biggest human moments are not understood yet:
The moment when life starts and the moment when life finishes.
The time between birth and death, the time of our living,
We dedicate to searching for our soul's salvation
To overcome pain and heavy temptations.

# BROKEN WINGS

My soul is broken, but my bones still stand strong.
Strange creature am I who breathes air.
Where is gone my life?
I ask myself . . .
How have my years vanished?
I ask myself, again . . .
They evaporate in a faraway sky.
I lost in life everything I could lose.
My screams from darkness, no one could hear.
Once light came out, it made blisters all over me.
I stayed as unprotected, unloved,
And abounded woman one.
My wounds will never heal.
They are so deep, even my bones are wounded.
What kind of life could there still be for me?
I lost my soul . . .
My wings and dreams are broken . . .
Is a future possible when the past does not exist?
Only desperate hope for his love is left.
But he does not want to love me like that.
Who would love a woman with broken wings?
One who cannot fly?
Who would love a woman without a soul?
I wish that I was already dead,
But for me, not even God has a mercy.

I am left to live like that
And hold these broken wings of mine.

# SWORD

The strength of my soul could move the biggest ocean waves.
My heart belongs to the stars,
Where my dreams live.
My life is like a wind disappearing through time.

My blood is pure black
From wounds, life-cuts.
My mind has turned into a mountain from life-burns.
My heart has become hidden;
It is wounded and everyone wants a cut.

My life is lonely
Because I accept that I will live my life without love.
I walk heavy steps forward.
I am pulling the burden of blackness behind myself.
But I walk forward . . .
I cannot kill the desire for light and to have love.

Still, this sword I carry in both of my hands
Is my only life.
I bow in front of God at the end of each day and say:
I desire Love,
But I am choosing to live with a sword.
Love made me weak.
This sword will give me power and make me strong.

Thank you, dear God, for my sword.
Please keep my arms strong.

# CHILD FROM A BLACK NIGHT

What on earth happened
When, for the first time, I opened my lungs and let out the screams?
What happened on the night this?
Did all the stars hide and the moon become dark?
Did life predict my destiny dark?

Did sky let thunder light the night and tears wash grass green
To support my devastating cry?
What happened when I first walked inside my many dark nights,
When I started to fulfil the black prophecy of my life?

Cry, cry on the sky, our Holy Mother, for us.
Cry for your children, who became lost and never see stars in the sky.
So, darkness swallowed our lives and we became lost
Inside a labyrinth of black nights.

To spread arms, open the lungs, and inhale the air.
To break loneliness and find salvation from darkness and isolation
became a dream for millions of us.

Because of living in dark nights without the stars,
Millions of souls cry through black nights.

# FRAGILE

Fragile soul, fragile heart . . . Broken mind . . .
While my body remains, my soul is lost forever.
Somewhere far away, it wanders,
Lost in places where grass is forever green,
Where flowers bloom year round.

It wanders with loves never lived,
Loves found living life only to become lost all over again.
If I cut my wrist, sand would be spilled;
If I opened my chest, my heart would cry,
It would let out the sound . . .
Please make me die . . .

What kind of life is mine?
Everything I had in my life left me.
My soul left me, too, because it does not want to live
With a fragile heart where tears instead of rain
Water dry flowers.

What kind of fragile person is to live?
One where the only heard sound is broken heart cries . . .

# REJECTED

A dream lived, a life where sorrow
Does not exist.
Once awake, I found myself
All grown up in a dark night and lost.
I started to pray .
and pray , and pray.
With time I redeemed my life,
But my heart was left behind in a dark night,
Beating in the chest of small, lost girl.
A girl who was a little nestling
Trying hopelessly to fly . . .
Lost without a mother, without a father,
I decided to become a child of God
And found there my home.
If I could forgive,
I would grow up and have a fly.
I would not be a nestling anymore.
I could have a family and my own home,
But how?
I have never belonged to anyone.
This is how my destiny gets written:
I wake up one day and stop dreaming.
God opens his door for me
He provides me with shelter,
But I do not find peace.
When my heart gets damaged, I stop growing,
In a body of woman, I forever stayed
A hurt little girl.

# REBORN

In the deepest sorrow, when the eyes cry
And the heart weeps,
We lose our lives
And find ourselves at the bottom of the ocean of life.
We live life as a river does—without a clear flow,
Losing track inside time.

When darkness swallows life,
Illness is born, which makes us live our lives alone.
Illness does not accept companionship from the living,
So once illness takes hold of life,
The only thing that gets a place in our life is sorrow.

In illness we can't see the sun or get warm.
Our bodies become frozen cold.
In illness stars do not shine .
Our soul cannot see anything, because
It starts to live in the dark once the heart closes its doors to love.

In illness only God can feel and see
What our heart and mind
Are dealing with . . . how lost and isolated we have become.
We pray for heaven to open the door
For our sin to be forgiven.
We cry for everything that the heart missed in life.

When illness takes over life, we forget about pain.
We only want to close our eyes with peace of mind.
In my illness I gained peace of mind, and sins were forgiven,
But it took a long time for my heart to find a way
To escape from dark nights.
It makes me cherish every day of my new life.

# PLACE WITHOUT LOVE

A place without love
Is a place on Earth where our minds become black.
It is a place on Earth where colours get lost.
It is place on Earth where love cries.

Find me in this place, and bring me your love back.
Make sunshine and sky blue come again.
My love calls to you with language that flowers speak,
With language that makes butterflies fly.

Find me in my loneliness, where I sit
In my bravery and cry
In the place where dreams are waiting to be born.
Find me where I am waiting for your love.

Your love will bring beautiful colours into my heart.
It is going to make sunshine and flowers grow.
Your love is going to make millions of rainbows
Throughout this grey sky.


Your love is magic.

# SOLITUDE

My life is rain from the sky.
My life is millions of tears from my eyes.
Just as the sky with millions of drops of rain,
My eyes shed millions of tears from my heart.

My smile was stolen; only tears stayed mine.
Tears became comfort through pain and sadness.
Everything in my life was destroyed, damaged until
Tears became my only companions.

Tears, diamonds from my heart that stay forever mine .
They never leave me or dry up.
While standing next to a window with tears on my face,
I look at life passing slowly.
I observe a world of pain and suffering from this solitude of mine.

In my solitude, I can see reflections of many women
who's lives I have lived,
When in reality I've only been one lonely woman.
One who never lived or was alive.
I choose solitude for my life now;
There I found who I am.

In my solitude, my tears can fly like rain,
My heart can beat like thunder from a dark sky.
My solitude is my secrecy .
In my solitude, I can be who I really am and live a life of my own.
People try to break the walls of this solitude
in which I hide ,
Not wanting to be found.

I do not want to hurt anymore .
My solitude is my sacred.

# LABYRINTH

I wonder about life, then I think about what it means to die.
Where does life start, and where does it finish?
What to call this time in-between?
Is it sorrow, is it happiness, is it all mixed
In a jar to become something we call "our life"?

The place where the sun rises and a time when life gets born .
Is this place where magic becomes alive?
Then we start to walk
In order to find love and conquer life,
To escape pain and temptation,
To find salvation.

Salvation, we all desire,
For something called "life".
Some of us find it in love, some in kindness, and some find it
In evil that destroys faith and does not assure light;
They let life become a dark night without the moon or stars.

Some are lucky to be born
With stars that shine for them throughout nights.
Some find it waking, having stepped through darkness.
Some spend life looking for this salvation.
Some hearts drown in a dark cemetery.
They get stacked forever in a dark graveyard.
Alive or dead, for them life becomes the same.

# HONEY AND BEES

Your words that were never said -
Your kisses that never touched my skin .
Everything disappeared in the river of life.
Only the shadows of my dreams were left.
The shadows of my love were never real
Or destined to live.

My life disappeared, too.
Got lost somewhere far away, carried by the wind of life.
It vanished like drops of rain from the sky.
Only the shadows of pain were left to haunt me
Through the dark nights of living.

I wish my poems had never been written.
They are all about what my heart missed in life:
About the pain my wounded heart
And broken mind endured.

Still, people do not allow me to heal, to move on.
My heart becomes honey for all the bees,
Attacking the steams of my heart,
Trying to suck out the love and get a taste.
They are not capable of feeling or living,
But they cannot stop obsessing and dreaming.

I wish to forget all
Who claimed how much they loved me,
Just to break me over and over again,
Never having the intention of stopping . . .

# IN SEARCH OF PEACE

In her solitude, she found peace.
She closed her eyes and she could feel
Her heart become healed.
She closed her eyes and she saw the most
Beautiful flower fields under blue skies.

How strong she became.
After years of pain, she felt that her heart
Became whole and pain-free.

God's love healed her
While people's love made her ill.
For the first time in her life, she was happy.

She took the crown from her head and added a scarf.
Gold and love she decided to give the world.
For herself she decided to keep
Peace in her mind and faith in her heart.

# LONELINESS

My heart: only one more shining star
Lost in the dark blue sky, expecting to fall and stop shining.
My cry sounds through nights,
Echoes of a samurai sword that crosses my lonely life.

My desire for love
Only one wish more in the ocean of my wishes.
You, my love, tsunami wave of my life and my biggest unfulfilled wish
In the land of my secret dreams, you become.

My heartbeats
Endless echoes of my life, as powerful as drum sounds.
I cross my days and nights in the lonely desert of living while
My heart beats and confirms that am I still alive.

My life
Sorrow buried in the depth of my heart.
Life behind the curtain of tearful eyes. My living is
A dream, a mystery marked by my unfulfilled human desire
To love and be loved.

# LIVING FEARLESSLY

When life is a tunnel of night without stars ,
When life is pain and sorrow ,
Fear disappears, and when you see a wolf
To you is lamb from the sky.

When life is a dark night without stars,
There is no difference between day and night.
Fear becomes your power.
You stand and, with bravery, walk streets that are empty.
You think it is destiny that cursed your life?
You befriend a black wolf in the loneliness of a dark night—
The only one who is not afraid of a cursed life.
It walks with you through life.
There is nothing to fear, so nothing is to lose, nothing to risk,
Because in darkness and loneliness,
Everything has already been lost.
Only the desire to survive is left.
Hope that is the same as a lost star on dark sky
Could pop up and cross with its shine endless black nights.

When life is a dark night, fear becomes your power.
It empowers you with strength
To walk ahead and rise up to the sky to reach the sun.
You start to live fearlessly with a heart
The same as the one that beats inside the black wolf.
One that rules day and night, world and human minds,
With energy empowered straight from the sky.

When you survive dark nights, you become
The human whose chest beats with the powerful black wolf heart . . .
One who is not scared to walk the streets of a cursed life.
You become a human who starts to live fearlessly in your life.

# NOSTALGIA

When I look back at my past, I cannot see anything.
Only emptiness.
Still, my past life is alive inside of me.
My life disappeared like snow melted by the touch of spring sun.
I suppose only nostalgia stays in me, keeping that past life alive.

Nostalgia for the time when my heart was pure and happy—
When I could look high into the sky and see beauty.
A time when I was looking forward to living life and growing up.
Nostalgia for this time of innocence is left in my heart.

Still, if I could return to this time, would I?
Only dreams that were pure . . .
My nostalgia is not for a past and happy life,
But for the innocence that was lost, that existed in the past.
Nostalgia for the peace of pure feeling from the heart—
It has disappeared forever,
like white snowflakes melted by the first touch of spring sun.

Now a feeling of melancholy lives in me. I call it nostalgia .
I wish I never grew up and my heart stayed forever pure.
But it is not the way life it is meant to be, or the way we die.
Everything melts and disappears in time, as with snow,
As do we.

I let my tears glaze my face,
Because I see how, in a faraway past,
The snow of my life was crystal white and clear.
Nostalgia is left for this time

When everything was white, pure, and clear.
Time and life can't be brought back or lived all over again.
Once things melt, they are forever gone.

It is a lucky person who manages to preserve pieces of this childhood innocence.
Mine is gone forever, destroyed from living a hard life.
My life became nothing similar to the one
That I imagined as a child, with a pure heart looking at the stars
That shined at night, high above in the sky.

Only nostalgia is left now .
Nostalgia for the piece of life that was crystal white and clear as snow,
But disappeared forever in the time of growing up.

# ORANGE DESERT

In the middle of desert, my soul lives, and my heart beats.
With the orange desert sand on all sides of world, I am thrown.
I do not know which direction the wind pushes me—
From west to east, from north to south, I am pushed.

I am a grain of orange desert sand
Carried by the wind and thrown to all sides of the world.
Where my heart will stop, I do not know.
Hopefully somewhere where my soul will find a piece of peace.
It is what I dream at night.

My soul cries in this orange desert. I am no one .
Still, there is so much pain in my heart, and my soul weeps.
I try to understand my life.
Where did all of this come from? How did I end up in deserted?

While the sun burns my soul,
The unmerciful wind breaks me, too.
I ask myself: why finish me like this?
To God in my lonely nights, I whisper.
He is the only one who hears my crying, my praying and hoping
For my heart to grow back wings and fly once more.

Am I so invisible I do not even know I am alive?
I am a grain of sand in an orange desert of life.
Pain and suffering are the only things that remind me of feeling alive.
The only sound that breaks the quiet desert is my loud heartbeat.
Still, from far away, I hear cries. I feel pain, even though it is not mine.

I am a person who does not have a family.
I am a human who does not have a country.
Lonely and neglected, my heart is in the desert of living,
Where I hear millions of souls cry for help.

# WHITE DOVE

Blinded loves.
Blinded lives.
Hearts full of pain.
What is left inside the black night to give us light?

Life desires turn into empty dreams.
The people we love . . .
Strange souls and passing visitors
Through the emptiness of our living.

Painful minds
Stuck inside a labyrinth of darkness.
Heavy bodies walk forward in hope
That minds will reach the light.

Tied-up hands—nothing to give.
Nothing to take back.
Nothing to use these tied hands for.
What sustains is only that lives and souls
stay tied up with ropes of pain.

Everything that is beautiful melts.
Disappears into black soil.
Only the chains of pain are left tied to
Empty lives, painful hearts, and broken dreams.

O' dear God, please release a white dove
To spread its wings and bring light across our dark sky!

# ENCHANTED

*Inspired by Mozart Symphony No. 40*

In enchanting wood, she is lost .
She is running . . . faster and faster .
She is trying to find way out .
It is completely dark—no stars in the sky.
A labyrinth of dark memories swallowed her life.

Only a fading memory of love from his eyes
Keeps her alive inside this deep darkness, but
If he would really love her, his eyes would shine light
Through her dark nights, through her enchanted life.

She would come to him and find love.
Her curse would be broken, and she would not be
Enchanted, anymore .

*O' desperation . . .*
*O' my desperation . . .*

It is pain! It is sorrow! It is blackness!
She takes a knife ! She cuts her wrists and spills blood!
She is spilling red blood inside her black night.

She is killing her enchanted life.
She will never have his love -
What is the point of her being alive and living this life?
She smiles sadly and slowly closes her tired eyes.

Her lips whisper one last thing:

Once you find me in this enchanted wood,
Do not cry or be sad, my dear mother.
You never stand next to me or share in my life's journey.
Tell me: Why would I keep myself alive?
My soul stops crying, so my heart from sorrow becomes dry -
Nothing is left for me to live for.
I will be happy where I am going.
My soul always wondered and dreamed
About living in the night sky between shine stars .


Death is not the worst thing for her.
It became her saviour from dark nights and an enchanted life.
After all, she was not enchanted in deep dark wood.
She was neglected and left to cry inside the depth of the blackest nights.

# DESTINED TO BE UNLOVED

To open your heart and mind,
Trying to find salvation and break loneliness
Became the unfulfilled dream of my life.
It was the weeping scream from far away darkness
I found myself living in.

Why does God not hear my cry?
Why does he not hear the cries of all of us?
Are we not all his children?
I wonder whose sins I am paying to live this life?
A life of hurt and abandonment, and one where
I am so unloved?

My faith is born by praying.
Still, there are moments I ask myself:
Whose decision is it for me to live this life?
Is there light in this dark life I am living?
Is there the light of hope for millions of people
Who are living life the same as I am?

After all, what are we all?
Only single grains of sand in an infinity of sand.
Only single grains of sand in a desert dune.
We are all destined to get lost in infinite time—
Is that what all of us are?

Each of us has a destiny of our own.
Maybe our lives are not God's decision after all.
However, we need faith to find meaning of our lives.
If only there was an answer for why my mother never loved me?

If I could find an answer on this same as I found faith?
When is the time for me to die in peace,
Without any questions on my mind?

# SOLIDARITY POEMS

# PARALLEL LIVING

In deepest sorrow, the heart weeps.
In deepest sorrow, our lives and souls become lost.
We weightlessly sink
To the deep bottom of life's ocean.

Our life becomes a muddy river without a clear flow—
That lost direction and track with time.
Deep sorrow is the only thing we feel in our lives,
So when sorrow takes life, everything else surrenders,
And darkness swallows life.

Nothing can breathe next to sorrow .
Illness is born, which make us live life alone;
Illness does not accept companions in living.
So once illness takes life,
The only thing that gets placed inside our lives is sorrow.

In illness, we can't see the stars or be warmed by the sun.
Our bodies become frozen cold.
Our souls cannot see anything, because
They start to live inside the dark
since our hearts closed their doors to any love.

Our minds start to cry for everything our hearts missed
But would bring happiness inside our life . . .
When illness takes over life, we forget about pain.
We only want to close our eyes with peace in mind.

Some people survive it, but for them,
The stars and sun rarely shine again.
Once inside the coffin of sorrow,
The heart gets swallowed by eternal dark .
Our bodies, alive, become a soil , a place for
Dreams lost and never lived to grow
As flowers seeded by our time living.

Our lost or missed dreams become pieces of us
That we start to witness as lost parts of us
In some parallel life.

*Poem written out of compassion for people*
*who are affected by any kind on mental suffering.*

# TRAPPED

I left my home. I left my country.
My thoughts stay there, but pain goes with me.
My pain follows me alongside my hope to find peace.
My pain accompanies my desperations.
I do not know if life is worth living.
Still, I want to breathe and be alive.

Do not cry, lost child of mine either.
My love is wide; it will find your heart wherever you are.
From far away, my love covers and protects that little body of yours.
I am your mother. I am your hope.

I am something you come from.
You can't ever go too far from me and my love.

Pray for my soul not to lose strength.
Pray for the world to become better place,
For a world where my child will not cry.
Where the sun shines and stars spark.
Here I will pray for the millions of us who left our homes!

We search to find a safe place beneath the sun.
We search for a place where flowers grow.

We search for a place where we will be together with our children.
It is our dream to have a simple life:
A roof over our heads where the sun shines during the day,
And where we can see sparks of stars during the night
Instead of the lighting strikes of devastating war.

*Poem inspired by the Syrian refugee's crisis,
or anyone who has been displaced from what they call their homeland.*

# SREBRENICA: BOSNIA AND HERZEGOVINA

A desperate mother above her son's grave, shedding tears.
Heaven's flowers grew on her son's grave.
She is crying and letting her tears water the black soil
And grow green grass on the place
Where her soul is buried in eternal rest.

She lives her life, but she doesn't breathe anymore.
She has eyes, but has become blind from pain and sorrow.
She has a heart, but it does not beat or feel anymore.
She is alive, but her life is buried under black soil
Next to her son in eternal rest.

Her mind silently cries . . .
Should I pray? Should I God on punishment call?

Should I forgive so they will burn in hell?
God will already punish them.
Then again, am I to be only a mother who is left to live
While her soul is forcefully taken and covered with black soil?
There are so many of us who are shedding tears
Above this black soil.

Neither can I die or forgive . . .
Desperate mother that I am .

*Poem written to acknowledge the genocide of Bosniak people in Bosnia and Herzegovina. This event was the biggest genocide since World War II and occurred under Slobodan Milošević and Radovan Karadzic rule in Serbia and Bosnia and Herzegovina. These rulers misled their own people and brought disaster on both countries, which became a worldwide issue.*

# IN GOD'S HANDS

Is life a black-and-white picture of God's painting?
Do we create it ourselves through black-and-white living?
Why are the colours of life disappearing?

When we reach the bottom of hell or rise back up to sky,
Does it make a difference in our black-and-white living?
Should we pray, kneel, and ask God for forgiveness from our sins?

Do we have right to?

Will God hear our cries, because faith is abounded?
Will he open the door for our lost souls, feed our hearts and minds
With blessings of forgiveness?
Can we find faith and make love alive again?

If only we knew how and where faith was lost,
Maybe we could find it again.
Life could start again with God's praise
And dedication to human morals and values.
We could be happy and live in love with each other again . . .

*Poem inspired by the devastating consequences of war,*
*which cause the biggest of human anguishes and are a time*
*when the ethics and morality of people are heavily tested.*

# FIELDS OF WHEAT

Before the horizon where life meets death,
In search of a peace soul like lost butterflies fly.
In a field of golden wheat that becomes sacred bread,
Lost souls have butterflies that fly and cry.

Some lost soul is spreading their wings there
For the peace it desires.
I hear its voice . . . I recognise the sound
Of its cries, which through eternity fly to my mind and say:

*Help . . .*

I see serenity, but I cannot reach it there.

Open the blue sky and accept one who has become lost.
At the door of your heaven, millions of souls cry.
Those who are victims of violence die and become forgotten . . .

Blow the wind and make waves
In these fields of golden wheat .
I wonder and cry for someone's soul
Who weeps and waits for you to open the door.

Everything in this world is easier than loosing people you love.
How they are living their lives in pain and are forever lost . . .
What good is it for me to know that my soul is found
When every night I hear the cry of nearby souls who have lost their love?

*O', Holy Mother,*
*Forgive us our sins. We are born clean,*
*But who could live life and stay clean, not to sin?*
*Sinners we become*
*In depth of sorrow, in depth of lives lost.*

In the middle of your golden field,
I am kissing your soil black.
This is the place where my soul is born,
Where my body grows.
My tears water your fields of gold
While I live my life thinking I am forever lost . . .

*Poems inspired by innocent people who lost their lives and became war victims.*

# IF MY TEARS COULD REALISE MY PAIN

If my tears could realise my pain,
If they could help my wounds heal,
If they had the strength and power of my pain,
I would be a free woman now.
Hurt and pain would get out of my life,
Released and washed by the millions of tears
My heart lost.

If my tears meant anything
In this world of cruelty and loss,
My heart would become crystal clear.
There would not be pain and wounds left.
In my heart and mind, everything would become
Released and washed by the millions of tears
My heart has lost.

My tears are a silk river, a streaming falls
My squashed heart drips.

My tears are the warm sun burning my face.
My tears do not make anything easier in my life.
They are just showing my desperation and fears.
My tears show my life exodus and fears.
This is what my tears do.

My tears, my heart-squashed drops, sun-warmed and dried, . . .
They do not make anything better in this world
Where people think only of greed.
It is not God who makes me suffer and fear,
But people who do not understand what it means
To fear and have a heart in pain.

*Poem inspired by people who have been the target of racial discrimination.*

# ABOUT THE AUTHOR

**Stacy Nicholson** is a poet, novelist, and humanitarian. Born in rural Bosnia, a former Yugoslavian Republic, Nicholson moved to Australia in 2002 as a war refugee. There she obtained a degree in Library Information Services and went on to build a successful career in Library Services, working at some of the most renowned libraries in Victoria.

Nicholson first became known for her romantic poetry with the book *Stay With Me*, but it did not take long for her writing in other genres to become equally popular and loved. In general, her writing has been described as reflections of on universal human experiences, feelings that describe from the full range of human emotions, from awe to wonder and tenderness, from agony to ecstasy.

Nicholson takes pride in writing about different topics and reflecting on the current state of the world and humanity. She is particularly passionate about raising awareness about mental health through her writing, and she hopes to promote understanding of this issue that affects so many, especially young people. This is why she is called an author for the new generation.

Nicholson has written three books: A poetry book, *Stay With Me*, and her autobiography, *Colour of My Heart*. Both were published in 2021. Mystic River is her third book published in 2022.

She is fluent in two languages: Serbian and English.

Nicholson currently resides in Melbourne, Australia.
Profession: Poet and author.
www.stacynicholson.com